WORLDVIEW GUIDE

PLATO'S REPUBLIC

W. Bradford Littlejohn

canonpress
Moscow, Idaho

Published by Canon Press
P.O. Box 8729, Moscow, Idaho 83843
800.488.2034 | www.canonpress.com

W. Bradford Littlejohn, PhD., *Worldview Guide for Plato's Republic*
Copyright ©2019 by W. Bradford Littlejohn. Cited page numbers come from
the Canon Classics edition of Plato's *Republic* (2016), www.canonpress.com/
books/canon-classics.

Cover design by James Engerbretson
Cover illustration by Forrest Dickison
Interior design by Valerie Anne Bost and James Engerbretson

Printed in the United States of America.

A free end-of-book test & answer key are available for download at:
www.canonpress.com/ClassicsQuizzes

Library of Congress Cataloging-in-Publication Data
Littlejohn, W. Bradford, author.
Worldview guide for Plato's Republic / W. Bradford Littlejohn.
Moscow : Canon Press, 2019.
LCCN 2019031404 | ISBN 9781944503833 (paperback)
LCSH: Plato. Republic.
Classification: LCC JC71.P6 L588 2019 | DDC 321/.07--dc23
LC record available at https://lccn.loc.gov/2019031404

19 20 21 22 23   5 4 3 2 1

CONTENTS

INTRODUCTION

It's a rare accomplishment when one of the first representatives of a genre also turns out to be one of the greatest. But so it is for the *Republic*. One of the earliest attempts to write a sustained work of philosophy, Plato's masterpiece is also one of the widest-ranging philosophical enquiries, continuing to inform our questions and our thinking when it comes to being, truth, beauty, goodness, justice, community, the soul, and more.

THE WORLD AROUND

The *Republic* is set in Athens, the beating heart of Greek culture, sometime during the long Peloponnesian War that ravaged the Greek world from 431 to 404 BC. Of course, you'd never know Athens was locked in a life-or-death struggle from the tranquil and leisurely philosophical discussion that unfolds through the pages of the *Republic*. Perhaps, however, the awareness that Athens was probably facing the twilight of its military and economic power lent a certain urgency to the discussion of what the justly ruled city ought to look like. Plato penned the *Republic* several decades later (around 380 BC) after the power of Athens had crumbled—its democratic constitution temporarily replaced by a group called the Thirty Tyrants, and his own teacher Socrates, the star of the *Republic*, unjustly executed in 399 BC by a reactionary restored democracy. Certainly for Plato, the search for the ideal city was no mere idle philosophical speculation.

Still, it was a pretty good time to be a Greek. To the east, the great Persian Empire which had absorbed Babylon, Palestine, Egypt, and Asia Minor was in terminal decline following its defeats by Athens and her allies in 479 BC. The last book of the Old Testament was being penned by Malachi as the Jews settled into a long period of relative peace and cultural insignificance under Persian rule. To the west, Rome was still just another city among the warring tribes of the Italian peninsula, its own day for dominion still far in the future. During the Golden Age that preceded the Peloponnesian War, Athens had boasted the greatest playwrights in the world (Aeschylus, Sophocles, and Euripides), its first historians (Herodotus and Thucydides), the father of medicine (Hippocrates), and the famous statesman and orator Pericles. And, of course, the first philosopher, Socrates.

Through his student, Plato, Socrates would exert a greater influence on Western history and culture than all the other great Athenians of his era combined. Socrates found his calling in response to the Sophists—Greek rhetoricians masquerading as philosophers who offered their argumentative services for hire, convinced that there was no objective truth and so wisdom just meant knowing how to get ahead in the world. In response, Socrates embarked on a quest for objective knowledge and morality that has inspired many millions since, including the fathers of the Christian Church.

ABOUT THE AUTHOR

Plato was born in Athens under the name Aristocles in 428 BC,[1] son of an Athenian nobleman named Ariston. The nickname Plato, meaning "broad," was supposedly given to him because of his broad shoulders, or perhaps his broad forehead. He encountered Socrates early in life and became one of his most devoted admirers until the latter's death in 399 BC. After this shattering event, Plato traveled around the Mediterranean to learn from other philosophers and returned to Athens to start his own school of philosophy, the Academy, where he taught until his death in 348 BC. His most famous pupil, of course, was the philosopher Aristotle.

---

1. As with most "facts" derived from ancient sources, even these basic claims are uncertain and disputed, with most of our biographical information coming from the *Lives and Opinions of the Eminent Philosophers* written by Diogenes Laertius over five hundred years after Plato's death.

Plato bears a curious relationship to the works he authored, of which there are at least twenty-five.[2] In none of them does Plato openly put forth his own ideas; rather, all are presented as dialogues, conversations between Plato's teacher Socrates and other Athenians or visitors to Athens. In nearly all of them, Socrates does most of the talking and seems to serve as something of the spokesman for Plato's own position, though it is rarely that simple. Of course, it's difficult to know how much of what "Socrates" says in the dialogues actually represents the historical Socrates, since Socrates never wrote any philosophy down. Plato's dialogues are the only window we have to Socrates's ideas, but Socrates's words in the dialogues are the main window we have to Plato's ideas—in fact, Plato himself never even appears as a character in any of the dialogues.

We are also unsure how much, if at all, the dialogues attempted to capture actual conversations that Socrates might have had. Many of them, generally classified as "Early" dialogues, read a lot more like real conversations, often ending inconclusively, and might have been based on particularly memorable arguments that Plato witnessed. Book I of the *Republic* looks a lot like many of these early dialogues. The "Middle Dialogues" tend to see real conversation replaced by one main speaker expounding a

---

2. The precise number is debated because, although thirty-six dialogues were once attributed to Plato, a number of these are of disputed authorship.

viewpoint (presumably Plato's), with other characters just asking questions. Most of the *Republic* seems to fit within this category. The "Late Dialogues" are the most complex and challenging, dissecting debated concepts with great detail and occasional tediousness.

WHAT OTHER
NOTABLES SAID

Perhaps the most famous assessment of Plato is the one that you will hear in almost any undergraduate course on philosophy—Alfred North Whitehead's declaration that "the safest general characterization of the European philosophical tradition is that it consists of a series of footnotes to Plato."[3] And certainly, it is difficult to think of a notable Western philosopher or Christian theologian who was not profoundly influenced by Plato, either as an admirer or in angry reaction against him.

Although great thinkers from St. Augustine in the fifth century to C.S. Lewis in the twentieth have proclaimed themselves great admirers of Plato, his reputation has taken a bit of a hit in more modern times. Lord Macaulay eloquently opined in 1832 that:

---

3. Alfred North Whitehead, *Process and Reality: An Essay in Cosmology* (New York: Free Press, 1929), 39.

> Assuredly if the tree which Socrates planted and
> Plato watered is to be judged of by its flowers and
> leaves, it is the noblest of trees. . . . But, when we
> look for something more, for something which adds
> to the comforts or alleviates the calamities of the
> human race, we are forced to own ourselves disap-
> pointed. We are forced to say with [Francis] Bacon
> that this celebrated philosophy ended in nothing
> but disputation, that it was neither a vineyard nor
> an olive-ground, but an intricate wood of briars and
> thistles, from which those who lost themselves in it
> brought back many scratches and no food.[4]

This is perhaps mild in comparison with the verdict of Karl Popper, who classed Plato as the first and greatest enemy of the "open society" and declared "his political demands are purely totalitarian and anti-humanitarian."[5] Popper was particularly hostile to the *Republic*, although according to Simon Blackburn "it is commonly regarded as the culminating achievement of Plato as a philosopher and a writer."

Indeed, it is precisely the *Republic*'s greatness that has generated such divergent assessments: "Over the centuries, it has probably sustained more commentary, and been subject to more radical and impassioned disagreement,

---

4. Thomas Babington Macaulay, "Lord Bacon," in *Critical and Historical Essays*, vol. II (London: Longman, Brown, Green, and Longmans, 1832), available at http://oll.libertyfund.org/titles/macaulay-critical-and -historical-essays-vol-2 (accessed August 6, 2016).

5. Karl Popper, *The Open Society and Its Enemies,* Vol. I: The Spell of Plato (London: George Routledge and Sons, 1947), 76.

than almost any other of the great founding texts of the modern world."[6] Few books in human history have established themselves as such essential reading for any educated person, such that it could be said that "always, someone somewhere is reading the *Republic*."[7]

6. Simon Blackburn, *Plato's Republic: A Biography* (New York: Atlantic Books, 2006), 7.

7. M.F. Burnyeat, "Plato as Educator of 19th-century Britain," in *Philosophers on Education,* edited by Amélie Oskenberg Rorty (London: Routledge, 1998). Quoted in Blackburn, 9.

SETTING, CHARACTERS, AND ARGUMENT

The Republic is set (aside from the opening lines) in the house of Cephalus, an elderly Athenian aristocrat who is on friendly terms with Socrates and who seems, although wise, relatively uninterested in intellectual pursuits. He heads off to the temple once he realizes he is about to be stuck in the middle of a philosophical debate. He hands off the discussion, which has focused on the meaning of the term *justice*, to his son Polemarchus, who quickly finds that a respectable traditional definition, borrowed from the poet Simonides, seems inadequate to stand up to Socrates's shrewd questions. Into the discussion leaps the sophist Thrasymachus, one of that group of pseudo-philosophers who taught aspiring politicians how to use skill in argument to build their power. Speaking persuasively for moral relativists from all ages, Thrasymachus seeks to argue that "might makes right," and thus so-called "justice" is either whatever powerful men define it to be for their own benefit (his first position), or perhaps the silly scruples held by weak men who are not bold enough to seek the benefits that come from a life of injustice. Socrates's debate with Thrasymachus, aided occasionally by his friend Glaucon, Plato's brother, is lively and goes through multiple rounds before Thrasymachus finally slumps down, defeated.

Although this might have been the ending for one of Plato's other dialogues, this *magnum opus* is just beginning. At the start of Book II, Glaucon pipes up to challenge Socrates anew: Perhaps it is true that injustice doesn't pay, but isn't this only because society frowns on it, and most wicked men aren't clever enough to get away with it? Persuade me, says Glaucon, that justice is better *in itself*, not just because of its social consequences. This is Socrates's prompt to launch into a discussion (or rather, exposition—from here on out, the dialogue is more of a monologue, with Glaucon and his brother Adeimantus taking turns to pitch softball questions and interject variants of "yes of course!"). The discussion's theme gives the dialogue its title: the just republic, the rightly governed city-state. The ostensible reason is so that, by seeing justice and injustice on a larger scale, we will have more insight into what constitutes justice and injustice in an individual soul. But it would not be fair to suppose, as many readers do, that this is just a pretense, and Plato really wanted to write a book of political philosophy all along. Rather, it seems clear that for Plato these two discourses—about the just soul and the just city—really are both equally important and thoroughly dependent on one another.

So, for the latter part of Book II through the first half of Book IV, Socrates sketches the ideal city, before returning to a consideration of the virtuous soul at the end of Book IV. Book V returns to a discussion of some details of the republic's laws, before turning to a lengthy treatment of the soul of the philosopher, the true lover of wisdom, and his place in the city. This takes us up through Book VII, which ends by turning back to a discussion of the educational curriculum in the republic. Books VIII and IX then offer a famous account of the different types of constitution—aristocratic (virtue-loving), timocratic (honor-loving), oligarchic (wealth-loving), democratic (pleasure-loving) and tyrannical—and the kinds of soul that correspond to them.

In none of the lengthy (and let's be frank, sometimes tedious) discussion is the lively debate of Book I forgotten, at least by Plato. Although it may feel like a detached prelude, it's more of a preview. Many arguments or observations first raised in Book I anticipate themes that are developed in the later books, and the fundamental challenge posed by Thrasymachus—*why bother being good?*—is always in mind, no matter how much it can fade from view amidst detailed recommendations for the educational policies of the republic or inquiries into the nature of being. Thus in Books IX and X, Plato has Socrates circle around at last to face the question head-on, via a thorough sketch of the miseries in store for the "tyrannical man," who follows unswervingly the course of self-interest recommended by Thrasymachus. Such a man, warns Socrates, is bound to be always at war with himself, those around him, and the gods, likely to die a violent death and sure to have a miserable afterlife.

WORLDVIEW ANALYSIS

Few books, even among the classics, can boast such a wide range of themes and questions as Plato's *Republic.* Nearly all the perennial philosophical questions receive significant attention in the work, as well as many other issues, which, although we might now think of them as belonging to more practical disciplines, were for the ancients important questions of philosophy as well.

Among the former are such philosophical questions as these ten: *Is there such a thing as objective morality? What motivates people to do good? What is the relationship between knowledge and right action? How can virtue be taught? How can we come to reliably know objective truth? If truth is knowable, why are so many people mired in falsehood? What is the source of order in the universe? What is the true nature of God or the gods? Is the soul immortal? What is the relationship between the individual and society?*

Among the latter are such practical questions as: *What constitutes a good education? What is the value of literature and art? How should property be regulated? What are the different kinds of political constitution? How do political societies decay or improve?*

As we consider Plato's answers to these questions, we may be tempted to do so with a critical, dissecting eye, trying to single out all of the ways in which Plato, from our Christian perspective, goes astray. And yet our first response, on comparing Plato to the Bible and the Christian tradition, should probably be to be impressed at how often he seems to grasp the truth about the world, or at least grasp some part of it, even if he also sometimes whiffs it rather badly.

Consider the very first philosophical question above, *Is there such a thing as objective morality?*—perhaps the fundamental issue of our own day. In the modern West, we face our own hordes of 21st-century sophists: Thrasymachi arguing that the rules of traditional morality are simply oppressive restraints meant to benefit the ruling classes, and that the clever man acknowledges no law but his own self-interest. Tempted as we might be to dismiss such relativism and selfishness as the inevitable product of a "pagan worldview," Plato shows us many arguments for responding to such relativism on the pagan's own terms. Indeed, his defense of the objectivity, beauty, and blessedness of justice even has a thing or two to teach us Christians.

Consider in Book II where Glaucon asks whether justice is one of those goods to be valued for its immediate pleasure, irrespective of its consequences (like eating ice cream), one of those goods that is *both* pleasant at the time *and* beneficial to us in the long run (like eating fruit smoothies), or one of those goods ito be valued for its consequences, although it is unpleasant (like eating broccoli). Clearly, he says, it is not the first, but does it fall into the last category, as most people suppose, or could it be one of those highest goods that falls into the middle category? The world around us, like Plato's world, is always trying to tell us that righteous conduct is in the last category—maybe it's good for you in the long run, but it's sure not much fun—and too often Christians accept that categorization and subconsciously echo it in our sermons and child-rearing. "Yes, you might miss out on the fun the world has to offer now, but you'll be rewarded in heaven." In the *Republic*, Socrates argues unapologetically that the just man lives more happily in the moment than the unjust, dies more happily, *and* is more happy in the afterlife. This certainly resonates with such teachings as those of the Psalms and Proverbs.

If we turn to the seventh and eighth questions above, the heart of Plato's theology (*What is the source of order in the universe? What is the true nature of God or the gods?*), we can see better why many of the Church Fathers thought of Plato as almost a forerunner of Christianity—although we can also see why Platonism proved so dangerous to the church. Consider first the passage toward the end of Book II where Socrates and Adeimantus discuss what stories about the gods should and shouldn't be allowed in their ideal city. Socrates is remarkably bold in his critique of traditional religion—indeed, if the historical Socrates ever spoke thus, we might not be surprised that one of the charges leading to his execution was "impiety." The famous stories of Greek mythology from Homer and Hesiod, says Socrates, cannot possibly be accurate depictions of the gods, for the divine nature is perfect and sinless, not petty, quarrelsome, and immoral. Indeed, he concludes that precisely because he is perfectly good, the true God cannot be the cause of all things, since God would not cause evil (Jewish and Christian theology cannot accept this oversimplified conclusion; hence the perennial "problem of evil").[8] Socrates further contends that "it is impossible that God should ever be willing to change, being, as is supposed, the fairest and best that is conceivable"[9] and that "God [is] perfectly simple and true both in word and deed; he changes not, he deceives not, either by sign or word, by dream or waking vision."[10] These sentences are eloquent testimony to the truth of Romans 1:19-20, that the "invisible attributes" of God "have been clearly perceived," even

---

8. Plato, *Republic*, trans. Benjamin Jowett (1888), from the Canon Classics edition (Moscow, ID: Canon Press, 2018), Sect. 379 (p. 68).
9. Sect. 381 (p. 70).
10. Sect. 382 (p. 73).

by pagans, "ever since the creation of the world." To be sure, some translations here have Socrates speaking about "a god" rather than "God," and it is not at all clear that Plato is here seeking to espouse a kind of monotheism. But he does clearly recognize that the divine nature must be quite different than the blasphemous portrayals of the pagan poets and indeed the whole Greek religious system.

A more explicit approximation to the biblical mono-theist account of God comes in the discussion of the "Idea of the Good" in Books VI and VII. First, Plato argues that the task of philosophy is to turn the eye of the mind away from the fleeting and changeable visible realities to the unchangeable intelligible realities or "ideas"—also translated "forms"—that are the basis for an orderly and rational universe. Then, Plato says that there must be a still higher reality that gives being to these forms. Just as the sun sheds light that makes all physical things visible and warmth that gives life to all living things, so there must be a being, a Supreme Good, that makes other truths know-able and other beings exist. It is this "Idea of the Good" that "imparts truth to the known and the power of know-ing to the knower," and is "more beautiful than both truth and knowledge." Indeed, "the Good may be said to be not only the author of knowledge to all things known, but of their being and essence, and yet the good is not essence, but far exceeds essence in dignity and power."[11] To this description Glaucon replies "By the light of heaven, how

11. Sect. 509 (p. 230).

amazing!" and later philosophers, both pagan and Christian, were likewise impressed and fascinated with Plato's description of this Being beyond being.

And yet there is much that is lacking in this highest being, compared to the biblical God. While the translation "idea" may be unhelpful in implying a subjective concept rather than an objective being (hence the popular use of the term "form"), "the Idea of the Good" is like an idea inasmuch as it is more of a supreme principle than an agent. It does not, from other writings of Plato, seem to be responsible for creating the universe, and it certainly does not intervene in it; one cannot imagine it breaking the cedars of Lebanon (Ps. 29:5) or upholding the widow and fatherless (Ps. 146:9), much less becoming flesh and dwelling among us (Jn. 1:14). Indeed, although Plato is perhaps not as responsible for a Gnostic contempt of the flesh and the visible world as is sometimes claimed, it is clear from the discussion in Book VI and later in Book X that he considers the things of the material world to be pale reflections of true reality, distractions more than objects of beauty and wonder in their own right.

But what about the issues for which the *Republic* is most infamous? These may be grouped under the heading of our tenth question above: *What is the relationship between the individual and society?* Plato's republic is, after all, a long way off from the American republic, or anything we might recognize as a just and desirable society. When Adeimantus interjects at the beginning of Book IV that the rulers of Socrates's perfect city are not likely to be very happy, Socrates replies, "our aim in founding the State was not the disproportionate happiness of any one class, but the greatest happiness of the whole."[12] That does not sound too unreasonable when phrased that way, but most of us know enough history to know that little good ever comes from states that have no hesitation sacrificing individual happiness for "the greatest happiness of the whole," and the exposition that follows in Books IV and V is likely to increase our alarm.

Plato's republic is one in which traditional gender distinctions are abolished, as is traditional marriage (in favor of shared sexual partners), and the traditional family (in favor of state-raised children who will call all rulers their fathers and mothers), as well as private property. At least this would apply to the ruler and soldier classes. The craftsmen and farmers, who make up the majority of the city, will still live relatively traditional lives, but will be almost entirely subject to the decisions of the guardians, who will tell a "noble lie" to ensure that the lower classes think their lowly position owes to their inferior race. There is plenty here to offend the sensibilities of both the strictest conservative and the most eager progressive nowadays. However, Plato's abolition of traditional gender and family roles is not proposed in order to further individual liberty, as in the modern West (on the contrary, Plato is scathingly critical of such democratic libertinism in Book IX), but to ensure

---

12. Sect. 420 (p. 118).

a single-minded devotion to duty, patriotism, and the good of the whole.

And you have to admit, once you get over your instinctive revulsion, that Plato has a point. After all, the downfall of most political societies through the ages has been the self-interest of rulers, who have always been tempted to use their power to help expand their own private wealth or to build dynasties of power for their children and their favorites. The only way that Plato can think of to prevent this partiality and corruption is to insist that the rulers in his city may claim no wealth or children of their own, but learn to consider the shared resources of the city as the only property that they need, and the people of the city as the only family that they need. Each, he thinks, can learn to care for the needs of everyone as if they were his own.

You may even notice that parts of this look an awful lot like the New Testament description of the church, a society in which "no one said that any of the things that belonged to him was his own, but they had everything in common" (Acts 4:32), and in which "there is neither Jew nor Greek, there is neither slave nor free, there is no male nor female, for you are all one in Christ Jesus" (Gal. 3:28). Indeed, the church is, if anything, more radical than the republic, for even Plato could not imagine a society without the slave/free and the Greek/non-Greek distinction. The church is a society that seeks to live out many of Plato's aspirations of a community defined not by personal desires and interests, not by thirst for wealth or power or glory or pleasure, but by dedication to justice, truth, and the mutual good of all.

However, the biblical picture of the church recognizes that this community is far from its full realization, and always will be in history—for now, it remains constrained by the conditions of materiality and fallenness. Thus Christians still make use of private property, even while saying that nothing that belongs to us is our own, they still have husbands and wives even while recognizing that all are equally the bride of Christ, they still have parents and children even while embracing each other all as "brothers and sisters."

Plato's mistake is that of many Christian heretics, and many pagans: immanentizing the eschaton—that is, trying to make the transformed life of the new creation happen *now*, without a realistic assessment of the limitations of human nature as we now find it. This radical urge has been a perennial temptation in the history of the church itself, so we should be quicker to learn soberly from Plato's mistake than dismiss it as the ravings a communistic pagan. Indeed, many of the errors that we will find in Plato have appeared also in many Christian heresies, sometimes because of Plato's influence and sometimes just because "there is nothing new under the sun." Accordingly, Plato is one of those great thinkers who gives us almost as much to learn from when he is wrong as when he is right.

QUOTABLES

1. "The unjust is lord over the truly simple and just: he is the stronger, and his subjects do what is for his interest, and minister to his happiness, which is very far from being their own. Consider further, most foolish Socrates, that the just is always a loser in comparison with the unjust."

   ~ Thrasymachus (Sect. 343, Book I; p. 23)

2. "The just man does not permit the several elements within him to interfere with one another, or any of them to do the work of others—he sets in order his own inner life, and is his own master and his own law, and at peace with himself."

   ~ Socrates (Sect. 443, Book IV; p. 149)

3. "Can there be any greater evil than discord and distraction and plurality where unity ought to reign? Or any greater good than the bond of unity?"

   ~ Socrates (Sect. 462, Book V; p. 171)

4. "The Good may be said to be not only the author of knowledge to all things known, but of their being and essence, and yet the good is not essence, but far exceeds essence in dignity and power."

    ~ Socrates (Sect. 509, Book VI; p. 230)

5. "In proportion as riches and rich men are honored in the State, virtue and the virtuous are dishonored."

    ~ Socrates (Sect. 551, Book VIII; p. 278)

6. "The excess of liberty, whether in states or individuals, seems only to pass into excess of slavery. . . . And so tyranny naturally arises out of democracy, and the most aggravated form of tyranny and slavery out of the most extreme form of liberty."

    ~ Socrates (Sect. 564, Book VIII; p. 295–6)

7. "Great is the issue at stake, greater than appears, whether a man is to be good or bad. And what will any one be profited if under the influence of honor or money or power, aye, or under the excitement of poetry, he neglect justice and virtue?"

    ~ Socrates (Sect. 608, Book X; p. 351)

21 SIGNIFICANT
QUESTIONS AND ANSWERS

1. Why is Thrasymachus such a skeptic about traditional moral norms and justice in particular? (Book I)

> Thrasymachus is profoundly cynical about the human behavior he sees around him. It seems to him transparently obvious that most people are out to pursue their own interest, and that this goes for the powerful at least as much as anyone else. Just as many people who have lost faith in the political system today, Thrasymachus thinks that political authorities pass laws just to benefit themselves. But rather than denouncing this, he concludes that even the attempt to denounce this presupposes a moral standard, and humans being what they are, why shouldn't we assume that this moral standard itself is simply the product of what some group of people have defined, for the sake of their own interest?

2.   Does Thrasymachus sound like a postmodern relativist? How so or how not? (Book I)

> One of the key features of postmodernism is its claim that all truth claims or objective value are simply thinly-veiled power claims. "X is good" is simply shorthand for "I want to impose X on you, in order to strengthen my power over you." Accordingly, postmodernism insists on questioning every kind of objective morality as little more than a tool of oppression, and like Thrasymachus's mocking analysis of the shepherd and the sheep, tries to see through anyone's claims to good intentions as just another form of self-interest. Thrasymachus clearly has much in common with these instincts, but his practical conclusion—that we should embrace the right of the strong to impose their will, rather than trying to prop up the weak—is more like that of the more uncompromising Friedrich Nietzsche than our current crop of postmodernists, who inconsistently cling to at least the one objective moral value that oppression of the weak is always wrong.

3.   Which of Socrates's arguments against Thrasymachus seems most compelling? (Book I)

> Socrates attempts a number of different strategies for refuting Thrasymachus, beginning by asking whether "justice" is always doing what the strong command or doing what is in their actual interest. While this looks like mere quibbling at first glance, it actually reflects very important points explored

later on in the book about what is truly in one's
best interest and the connection between ruling and
knowing the good. Socrates then goes on to argue
that every craft seeks the good of those whom it
serves; if medicine is that which enables doctors to
do good to their patients, virtue is that which enables rulers to do good to their subjects. Along re-
lated lines, he later argues that those who are good
at any craft seek to match the leading practitioners,
rather than outdo them, but unjust people always
try to outdo their peers—a sign of weakness, rather
than strength. Finally, he points out that the unjust
are divided against others and against themselves,
and hence cannot flourish or succeed as the just can.
Each of these arguments uses premises that will be
explored and fortified much further in later books
of the *Republic*.

4. What is the point of Glaucon's enumeration of three
   different types of good? (Book II)

Glaucon wisely observes that most of the time people do the good, or what they deem to be good for
them, grudgingly rather than willingly. It might be
good, but it's not necessarily pleasant, and so people
do it for the sake of the rewards to be gained or the
consequences to be feared; indeed, this is generally how we have to teach children to obey when
they are young. Is justice like this, profitable but
unpleasant, as many people seem to think, or is it
something actually pleasant? There are trivial goods
that are pleasant at the time but of no lasting profit,

and then the highest goods that are both pleasant
to do and rewarding in the long-term—enjoyable
and profitable. He wants Socrates to make the case
that justice is one of these highest goods.

5. What point is Glaucon trying to make with his tale of
Gyges and the ring? Do you find it compelling? (Book
II)

The story of Gyges is a kind of dystopian spin on
The Hobbit—or perhaps it would be better to say
that *The Hobbit* is a kind of utopian spin on the story of Gyges. To expound his point further (that justice sure seems like one of those things that people
do only to gain rewards or avoid bad consequences),
Glaucon tells a story he has heard about a man
named Gyges who discovered a ring of invisibility.
Rather than using it innocently to help him in his
adventures of benevolent burglary like Bilbo, Gyges
quickly realizes that he can now get away with petty
evils he never would have attempted before. Heck,
he can get away with bigger evils ... indeed, with
pretty much anything, if he's clever enough! As
good and evil deeds are suddenly separated from
the consequences that would normally accompa-
ny them—the result of those deeds being seen by
others—Gyges' incentive to act morally evaporates.
Gyges is not especially bad, mind you—this just
proves that "wherever anyone thinks that he can
safely be unjust, there he is unjust."[13]

---

13. Sect. 360 (p. 43).

6.   What does the discussion of the gods in Book II tell us about the nature of pagan religion? (Book II)

> This remarkable section of the *Republic*, where Plato deconstructs the errors of pagan mythology and seeks to show the true nature of the gods, should give us pause about making careless generalizations about pagan religion. To be sure, it is probable that your average Athenian was either credulously convinced of the traditional stories about the gods he had been taught, or else an apathetic skeptic who merely kept up religious appearances. But Plato's far-ranging insight into how far Greek mythology strayed from a true grasp of the divine nature is echoed by later pagan philosophers and gives us some sense of the breadth of pagan religious thinking.

7.   What does Plato consider the key elements of a good education, and why? (Books II-III)

> Plato's conception of education is very broad indeed, and he returns to consider the elements of education in his ideal city several times in the *Republic*. But it is remarkable in this initial discussion how much he singles out as central two things that we might consider quite ancillary: musical training and physical training. Even more surprisingly, both of these are valued chiefly as means to the end of moral formation. Good morals depend on knowing the truth about justice, to be sure, but they depend just as much on well-trained bodies and emotions.

8. How does the discussion of the ideal city help answer
    the original question about virtue? (Book IV)

    > In Book IV, armed with his three-tiered model of
    > the ideal city, made up of ruling guardians, soldiers,
    > and craftsmen, Plato returns to discuss the ideal
    > soul, which he thinks mimics this threefold order.
    > Reason rules over all by deliberating on the com-
    > mon good, the spirited emotions serve the reason by
    > opposing enemies without and restraining appetites
    > within, and the lower appetites serve the essential
    > functions of helping the body eat and reproduce,
    > but easily get carried away. The four cardinal virtues
    > (prudence, temperance, fortitude, justice) are all
    > found in the proper relationships between these
    > three elements.

9. Why does Plato argue that the guardians must have
    property, wives, and children in common? (Book V)

    > As was argued against Thrasymachus in Book I,
    > justice would seem to depend on harmony and
    > working together, rather than each seeking his own
    > interest. Plato is convinced that there is no way for
    > a city organized around the distinction of "mine"
    > and "thine" to avoid falling into selfish rivalry. Only
    > if those in power learn to think of one another as
    > brothers and sisters, sharing all things in common,
    > will they be able to genuinely work for one anoth-
    > er's good.

10. What is the difference between "opinion" and "knowledge," according to Plato, and how does this give us insight into his fundamental metaphysical convictions?

> Whereas knowledge concerns "what is," opinion concerns that "which is and is not." Change, in other words, is a tremendous obstacle to knowledge on Plato's conception, and the truest things must be those which are free from the change that particularity and physicality impose.

11. Why does Plato think that only philosophers can be good rulers? Do you agree? (Books V-VI)

> Because philosophers are passionately devoted to truth and will seek it wherever it is to be found, they alone have a chance of laying hold of absolute beauty and absolute truth. Accordingly, they alone can be said to have knowledge rather than mere opinion, able to understand the root causes of things, their interconnections, and the fundamental realities, which never change. When you think of it that way, who else would you want ruling your city? Of course, many might respond that Plato has failed to appreciate the distinction between theoretical knowledge and hands-on practical expertise, the latter of which may go further when it comes to politics.

12. How does Plato conceive of the Form ("Idea") of the Good?

> The Form of the Good "imparts truth to the known and the power of knowing to the knower," and is "more beautiful than both truth and knowledge." As the sun of the spiritual and intelligible world, it is the utterly transcendent being that grounds both epistemology (the study of knowledge) and metaphysics (the study of being). No wonder later Christians thought it sounded a lot like the true God.

13. What is the point of Plato's famous Cave Analogy? (Book VII)

> The Cave Analogy seeks to explain quite a number of things for Plato. In it, he gives a vivid image for the relation between the physical world that preoccupies us and the higher realities that philosophy explores. He also seeks to explain why it is that philosophy is so difficult, why philosophers have such a hard time when they re-enter the mundane world of politics, and why ordinary people think that philosophers are talking nonsense when they go on and on about ultimate truth.

14. Is the ideal society likely to last long? (Books VIII-IX)

> Its prospects sure don't look very bright. In a remarkably perceptive and farsighted analysis, Plato shows how the society oriented toward justice gradually decays over the generations into one obsessed

with honor and warfare, then into one obsessed
with wealth, then into a democratic mob rule that
values pleasure above all, and finally, into a tyranny.
All of this, he thinks, can be traced just as readily
in the gradual corruption of several generations of
individuals in a family line, from a just man to a
tyrannical one.

15. What can we learn from Plato's critique of the oligarchic society? (Book VIII)

If Plato's remarks about oligarchy (and its decay
into democracy) don't scare you when you look
around at the modern West, I don't know what will.
When we allow money-lovers the positions of rule
in our societies, they will, predicts Plato, form an
unholy alliance with the lower passions of the cit-
izens, encouraging intemperance and moral decay
since the intemperate will spend more and borrow
more, thus making the rulers richer.

16. Were you surprised by Plato's condemnation of democracy? What do you think of it? (Book VIII)

The equality and freedom which we today tend
to applaud as the great features of democracy are
precisely what makes Plato so critical of it. In a
democracy, "the individual is clearly able to order
for himself his own life as he pleases."[14] "Great!"
we might say. Without virtue as his guide, however,
this just means that each man will pursue his own

14. Sect. 557 (p. 286).

passions and idle preferences, pulled to and fro
by his desires, while the state as a whole will be
characterized by apathy and libertinism rather than
a commitment to justice. This certainly does sound
a lot like modern democracy.

17. Why is the tyrannical man more miserable than any
other? (Book IX)

One cannot improve on Plato's own summary: "He
who is the real tyrant, whatever men may think, is
the real slave, and is obliged to practice the greatest
adulation and servility, and to be the flatterer of the
vilest of mankind. He has desires which he is utterly
unable to satisfy, and has more wants than any one,
and is truly poor, if you know how to inspect the
whole soul of him: all his life long he is beset with
fear and is full of convulsions, and distractions."[15]
Plato then expands upon this description through
an analysis of the different faculties and pleasures
that the soul is capable of.

18. What is the basis of Plato's critique of the arts? Do you
find it compelling? (Book X)

Although we might think of the arts as characterized above all by creativity, Plato is more cynical.
They are nothing but imitation in his view, copy-
ing things they see in nature and in history and
presenting them for our amusement. But since the
objects of sensible experience are themselves only

15. Sect. 579 (p. 315).

copies of more fundamental, eternal realities (cf. the
Cave Analogy), this means that the arts can present
us only with a copy of a copy, and why would anyone waste their time trying to learn anything from
such a pale shadow?

19. How does Plato seek to prove the immortality of the
    soul? (Book X)

    His proof is simple but compelling. Consider the
    diseases that may befall the soul, which he has an-
    alyzed at length in the preceding books. Do any of
    them destroy the soul, cause it to fall apart entirely
    and cease to exist? Clearly they do not, even though
    we know many bodily ailments that do so to our
    bodies, and indeed to the bodies of all living things.
    If the worst scourges of the soul are still incapable
    of destroying it, it must be by nature indestructible
    and thus immortal.

20. What features of Plato's account of the afterlife are
    attractive and which are not? (Book X)

    In Book X, Plato returns to his attack on traditional
    pagan religion by arguing against the prevailing
    views of the afterlife that he saw in much Greek
    mythology. Death, he argues, is only something to
    be feared for the wicked; for the just it is a victory.
    This much may be Christian enough, but his sub-
    sequent remarks about cyclical reincarnation show
    how difficult it was for pagan thought to approach

the Christian notion of a resurrection to eternal
rest.

21. Is Plato naive about human perfectibility? (General)

With his attempt to establish a utopian society
built on mutual brotherhood and ruled only by
those who seek after truth rather than power or
earthly goods, it is easy to critique Plato as naive-
ly optimistic about human nature. On the other
hand, his dark chronicle of the gradual collapse
of the ideal city in Books VIII-IX reveals that
even he is skeptical that the republic he describes
could endure more than a few generations. He also
recognizes that virtue is one of the most difficult
things you can possibly seek to obtain, requiring not
merely intellectual enlightenment but discipline, the
right environment, and a very careful and thorough
education.

FURTHER DISCUSSION
AND REVIEW

Master what you have read by reviewing and integrating the different elements of this classic.

AUTHOR, SETTING, AND CHARACTERS

Be able to describe the relationship between Plato, Socrates, and Athens. Also be able to summarize what Cephalus, Polemarchus, Thrasymachus, Glaucon, and Socrates contribute to the discussion of justice.

ARGUMENT

Be able to discuss the trajectory of the argument in the *Republic* from Book I to Book X, connecting the nature of justice, justice as a good in itself, political philosophy, and philosophical questions of absolute truth and being, including the Cave Analogy and "ideas" or "forms."

PHILOSOPHICAL ISSUES

Be able to describe what this classic is telling us about the world. Is the message true? What truth can we take from the characters, argument, and philosophical questions discussed? What was the Republic's influence on western philosophy after it? Finally, be able to interact with the following philosophical and practical questions (or any others you've noticed) from this classic:

- Is there such a thing as objective morality?
- What motivates people to do good?
- What is the relationship between knowledge and right action?
- How can virtue be taught?
- How can we come to reliably know objective truth?
- If truth is knowable, why are so many people mired in falsehood?
- What is the source of order in the universe?
- What is the true nature of God or the gods?
- Is the soul immortal?
- What is the relationship between the individual and society?
- What constitutes a good education?
- What is the value of literature and art?
- How should property be regulated?
- What are the different kinds of political constitution and how do political societies decay or improve?

TAKING THE CLASSICS QUIZ

Once you have finished the worldview guide, you can prepare for the end-of-book test. Each test will consist of a short-answer section on the book itself and the author, a short-answer section on plot and the narrative, and a long-answer essay section on worldview, conflict, and themes.

Each quiz, along with other helps, can be downloaded for free at www.canonpress.com/ClassicsQuizzes. If you have any questions about the quiz or its answers or the Worldview Guides in general, you can contact Canon Press at service@canonpress.com or 208.892.8074.

Dr. W. Bradford Littlejohn is the President of the Davenant Trust and an Adjunct Professor of Philosophy at Moody Bible Institute—Spokane. He is the author of *The Mercersburg Theology and the Quest for Reformed Catholicity*, *Richard Hooker: A Companion to His Life and Work*, and *The Peril and Promise of Christian Liberty*, and is an associate editor for the journal *Political Theology*. He is also a part-time investment advisor with Covenant Investment Advisors, LLC. He and his wife Rachel have three children.